A is for Angel
A Christmas Alphabet and Activity Book

by Debbie Trafton O'Neal

illustrated by Jan Bryan-Hunt

Augsburg Books
Bringing Families Together
for Children & Families

To my family, John, Lindsay, Morgan, and
Shannon, and to all families everywhere.
Celebrate the gift!
—D. T. O.

For Amy and Bryan
—J. B. H.

A IS FOR ANGEL
A Christmas Alphabet and Activity Book

Large-quantity purchases or custom editions of this book are available at a discount
from the publisher. For more information, contact the sales department at Augsburg
Fortress, Publishers, 800-328-4648, or write to: Sales Director, Augsburg Fortress,
Publishers, P. O. Box 1209, Minneapolis, MN 55440-1209.

ISBN 978-0-8066-5121-7

Edited by Lois Wallentine

The paper used in this publication meets the minimum requirements of American
National Standard for Information Sciences—Permanence of Paper for Printed Library
Materials, ANSI Z329.48-1984. ⊗™

09   4   5   6   7   8   9   10

Dear friends,

I love Christmas! I love the smell of Christmas trees, singing Christmas carols, baking my family's favorite cookies, wrapping presents, and decorating my house! But most of all, I love the Christmas story that tells about the special night when baby Jesus was born.

This ABC Christmas book is a fun way to learn your ABCs and tell the Christmas story, but is also a starting point for making your own Christmas projects. Choose some of your favorite illustrations on these pages to inspire and guide you in creating your own special Christmas memories for this year—and for years to come!

Merry Christmas!

Debbie Trafton O'Neal

Aa

A is for the **angel** who first shared the news.

B for the birds,
awaiting their cues.

C is for COW, warm in the stable.

Cc

Dd

D for the donkey, sturdy and able.

Ee

E is for earth, needing God's peace.

Peace on Earth

F for the flock, warm in their fleece.

Ff

G is for **glory**, God's praise high above.

Gg

Hh

H for the shepherds' **hearts**, given in love.

I for the **innkeeper**

who opened the door.

J is for **Joseph**,

"Is there room for two more?"

K for the King, the Savior we know.

Kk

L

L is for light and the stable aglow.

M m

M is for Mary, who followed God's plan.

N for the newborn,
God's Son born of man.

O is for **Owl**, asking
"Who is born on this day?"

Oo

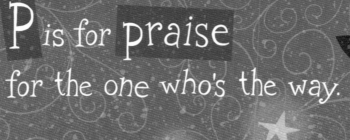

P p

P is for praise
for the one who's the way.

Q is for **quiet** as the town lay asleep.

R for **rejoicing** with news that won't keep!

Ss

S for the **star**
shining bright in the night.

T is for travelers
who followed the light.

T t

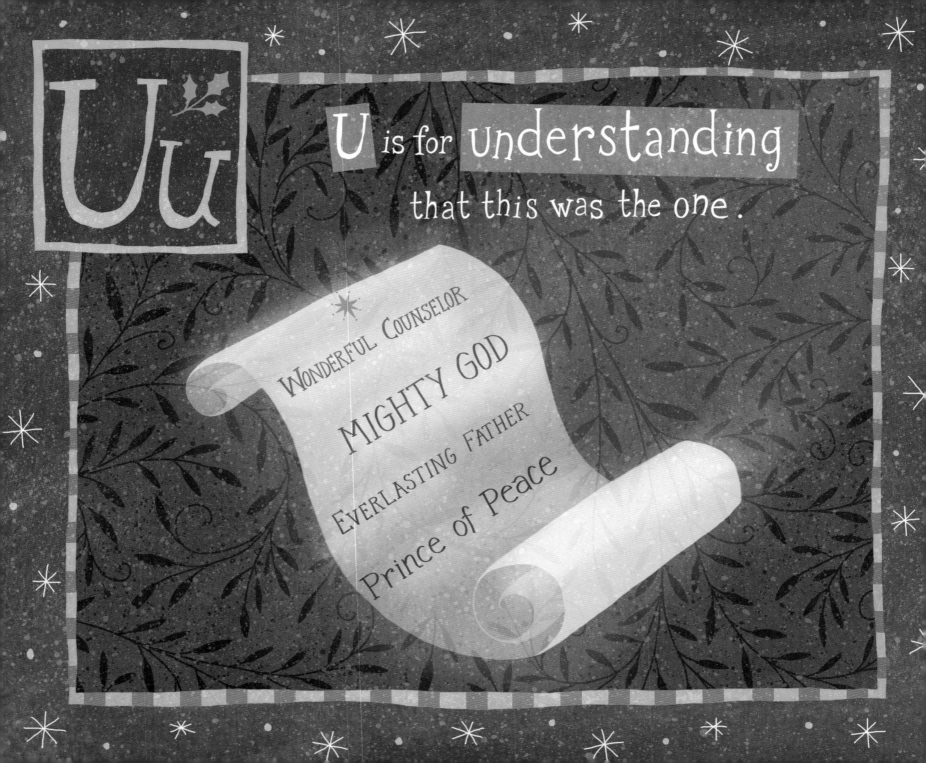

Uu

U is for understanding
that this was the one.

Wonderful Counselor

MIGHTY GOD

Everlasting Father

Prince of Peace

V for the VISIT with gifts for God's Son.

V v

W for the *wonder* of all who came by.

X is for exalting, praise lifted on high.

Y is for YOU, the reason
he came to stay.

And **ZZZ**'s from the baby, asleep in the hay.

Christmas Tree Skirt

The simplest way to make a Christmas tree skirt is to start with a solid-colored circular tablecloth. Cut a hole in the center, and a slit from one outer edge to the center hole. Recreate your favorite illustrations from this book, using felt or fabric and gluing or sewing the pieces onto the tree skirt. You could also draw your favorite shapes or objects that tell the Christmas story and paint them on the tree skirt with fabric paint.

How about using all of the elements of the story around the tree skirt to retell the Christmas story?

Christmas Stocking

Purchase or make large fabric stockings. If you use felt, it is easy to sew or glue the edges together. Add a loop for hanging, and a cuff at the top.

Let each person in your family choose a favorite part of the story and recreate that scene on his or her stocking. Cut the shapes from felt or other fabric that won't fray, and sew or glue the shapes to the front of the stocking. Don't forget to add each person's name to the stocking!

Gift Tags

Make or purchase simple manila gift tags to put on Christmas packages. Use the illustrations in this book to inspire your work and draw the people, places, or things from the Christmas story on your tags. Paint or color the tags with watercolors or felt-tip markers. Tie your tags on packages, use them as Christmas cards or invitations to a holiday party, or attach a row of them on a curtain rod or indoor clothesline to retell the Christmas story.

Baby or Mantel Blocks

Many families have a treasured nativity set. Let this book inspire you to make a set of baby or mantel blocks to play with that retell the Christmas story!

You can use sanded wood blocks or foam blocks that you can cut from foam purchased in a fabric store. Cut the people, places, and things from the Christmas story from felt or other sturdy fabric and glue to the blocks. Store all of the blocks on a mantel or in a wicker basket that can be turned on its side as the stable!

Peace On Earth

WONDERFUL COUNSELOR
MIGHTY GOD
EVERLASTING FATHER
Prince of Peace